Beyond .....s, Where

Ancient Mysteries Meet Modern

Adventure.

Uzbekistan

Vacation Guide 2023

Curtis Kerr

Table of Contents

INTRODUCTION

Excitement swept over me as I got off the aircraft onto the tarmac. I had reached Uzbekistan, a country with stunning natural beauty and a lengthy history. The historic towns that awaited my research were enchanted by the sun's golden-hued scenery.

As I set out on my expedition, I couldn't help but be filled with awe and curiosity as I searched for the secrets that were concealed beneath the elaborate blue domes and magnificent minarets. Time appeared to stand still in Uzbekistan, where the wind carried the whispers of bygone civilizations.

My adventure started in the vibrant capital city of Tashkent, which expertly combined heritage and technology. The bustling bazaars and impressive Soviet-era buildings provided a look into the country's rich history. From there, I traveled through the ancient towns of Samarkand, Bukhara, and Khiva as I followed the fabled Silk Road. I was in awe of the magnificent mausoleums, elaborately tiled mosques, and humming market squares as I walked through each successive historical period.

But Uzbekistan was more than simply a location of historic treasures; it also held the promise of a thrilling contemporary experience. I found myself trekking across stunning mountain ranges, discovering undiscovered caverns, and savoring the mouthwatering tastes of Uzbek cuisine.

As the days progressed into weeks, I came to understand that Uzbekistan was more than simply a place to visit; it was a captivating tapestry of hospitality, culture, and the arts. I was welcomed into the vivid world of the Uzbek people thanks to their warmth and friendliness.

Uzbekistan had won my heart despite its ancient secrets and blue domes. And as I embarked on my subsequent journey, I was aware that the impressions and encounters I had while in this remarkable place would remain with me always, fueling a lifetime passion for travel and discovery.

A landlocked nation in Central Asia, Uzbekistan is officially referred to as the Republic of Uzbekistan. Tajikistan, Afghanistan, Kazakhstan, Kyrgyzstan, and Turkmenistan are its neighbors to the north, northeast, southeast, and southwest, respectively. Uzbekistan, which has a population of nearly 34 million, is the most populated nation in Central Asia.

Uzbekistan's history dates back thousands of years, and the country was a significant junction on the Silk Road trading route throughout that time. The country's rich cultural past has been influenced by several civilizations, including the Persian, Greek, Arab, Mongol, and Russian empires.

Following its 1991 separation from the Soviet Union, Uzbekistan underwent substantial political and economic changes. The capital and biggest city of the nation, Tashkent, is governed under a presidential republic system.

Particularly the stately towns of Samarkand, Bukhara, and Khiva—all of which are listed as UNESCO World Heritage Sites—Uzbekistan is known for its architectural marvels. The mosques, mausoleums, and madrasas (Islamic schools) in these locations are exquisite examples of Islamic architecture.

The huge Kyzylkum Desert in the north and the Tian Shan and Pamir-Alay mountain ranges in the south make up the country's varied and stunning natural scenery. The verdant meadows and vibrant traditional crafts of the east's rich Fergana Valley are well-known.

A delicious blend of tastes that are inspired by Uzbekistan's position along the Silk Road may be found in its cuisine. The basics of Uzbek cuisine, including plov (pilaf), shashlik (grilled pork), and manti (dumplings), are loved by both residents and tourists.

Uzbekistan has seen an increase in tourism in recent years as a result of its ancient landmarks, welcoming people, and unspoiled natural beauty. The government has made investments in enhancing the country's infrastructure and marketing tourism, making it simpler for tourists to discover its undiscovered beauties.

Uzbekistan provides a one-of-a-kind and enthralling experience, whether you're fascinated by the historic Silk Road, anxious to immerse yourself in colorful bazaars, or yearning to explore the raw grandeur of Central Asia.

Why Go to Uzbekistan?

Rich Cultural Heritage: Some of the most remarkable and well-preserved architectural marvels of the old Silk Road may be found in Uzbekistan. Beautiful mosques, mausoleums, and madrasas are found in cities like Samarkand, Bukhara, and Khiva. These structures are decorated with elaborate tile work and decorative motifs. Exploring these historic locations gives visitors a window into the nation's interesting history and the chance to see UNESCO World Heritage Sites up close.

Untouched Natural Beauty: Uzbekistan is a nation with a variety of landscapes in addition to its old towns. There is a plethora of undiscovered natural beauty, from the enormous deserts of Kyzylkum to the spectacular mountain ranges of Tian Shan and Pamir-Alay. In the nation's national parks and protected regions, outdoor enthusiasts may partake in pursuits including hiking, camping, and animal observation.

Warm Hospitality: Uzbekistan is renowned for its warmth and friendliness. The locals are kind, and they often welcome guests. The ability to learn about local cultures, traditions, and ways of life via interaction with people enriches the vacation experience even more.

Culinary Highlights: The Silk Road trade route left its mark on the delicious taste mix that is Uzbek cuisine. The nation's cultural history is reflected in traditional foods including plov (pilaf), shashlik (grilled meat skewers), and manti (dumplings). For food lovers, visiting regional markets and indulging in regional cuisine is a joy.

Travel: Uzbekistan has worked hard to upgrade its tourist infrastructure in recent years. Travel throughout the nation is now more convenient and pleasant for tourists because of government investments in transportation, lodging, and services. In addition, the requirements for obtaining visas have been lowered for many nations, making it simpler to visit and explore Uzbekistan.

Festivals & Events: Throughout the year, Uzbekistan is home to several vivacious festivals and cultural gatherings. These festivals provide an opportunity to take in traditional music and dance performances as well as vibrant processions. Particularly noteworthy are the Navruz (Persian New Year) celebrations, which unite communities in exuberant celebrations.

In 2023, there will be a rare chance to go to Uzbekistan and see firsthand how smoothly traditional culture coexists with contemporary appeal. Uzbekistan offers visitors a memorable and genuine travel experience because of its rich history, stunning natural surroundings, friendly people, and delectable cuisine.

What to Expect from this Guide

The complete travel guide The Uzbekistan Vacation Guide 2023: Beyond the Blue Domes; Where Ancient Mysteries Meet Modern Adventure is created to help you get the most out of your vacation to Uzbekistan. This book gives you a general introduction to the nation, its cultural history, and the thrilling adventures that lie ahead.

The introduction to Uzbekistan in the guide highlights both its historical importance as a crossroads of civilizations and its position in Central Asia. It highlights the country's rich cultural legacy, untainted natural beauty, friendly hospitality, and the advancements achieved in tourist infrastructure to explain why 2023 is a great year to go to Uzbekistan.

The manual then digs into how to plan your trip, including details on how to travel to Uzbekistan, information on visa requirements, and advice on how to make the most of your schedule. It offers information on the ideal time to go, the suggested amount of time to stay, and how much money to save aside for your vacation.

The next step is a virtual tour of some of Uzbekistan's most popular attractions. You'll learn about the architectural marvels, UNESCO World Heritage Sites, and undiscovered jewels that each location has to offer, from the vibrant capital city of Tashkent to the breathtaking cities of Samarkand, Bukhara, and Khiva. Additionally, it draws attention to other locations that are less well-known but just as fascinating, such as the Nuratau Mountains, Termez, Fergana Valley, and Shakhrisabz.

The guide examines Uzbekistan's ancient history and culture to fully comprehend its attraction. The importance of the Silk Road, UNESCO

World Heritage Sites, and the thriving arts and crafts industry are all covered in depth. Additionally, it offers information on the celebrations, activities, and customs that you may take part in while there.

The guide also provides a peek at Uzbekistan's outdoor activities, food and drink scene, nightlife, retail, spa, and wellness opportunities for tourists looking for contemporary experiences. Everyone can find something to enjoy in Uzbekistan, whether they want to hike across stunning landscapes, enjoy local cuisine, or indulge in relaxing spa treatments.

The book then offers useful details on several types of lodging, including guesthouses, homestays, camping, and special lodgings in addition to hotels and resorts. It provides advice for picking the best lodging depending on your tastes and spending limit.

The book provides helpful advice for tourists, such as health and safety data, language and communication suggestions, currency and banking details, transit alternatives inside Uzbekistan, and customs and etiquette requirements, to ensure a smooth and pleasurable journey.

The book finishes with a summary of the best sights and activities, as well as concluding reflections and suggestions to motivate and direct you as you start your Uzbekistan journey. Additionally, it offers resources for more information, enabling you to learn more about the topics that most interest you.

You need the Uzbekistan Vacation Guide 2023: Beyond the Blue Domes; Where Ancient Mysteries Meet Modern Adventure to discover this fascinating country's treasures and make lifelong memories there.

II. PLANNING YOUR TRIP

Getting to Uzbekistan

There are various ways for people to reach Uzbekistan, and the process is rather simple. The main methods of travel to Uzbekistan are listed below:

1. By Air: Flying is the most popular and practical method to go to Uzbekistan. There are many international airports in the nation, with Tashkent International Airport (TAS) serving as the principal entry point. It has direct flights from several nations in Europe, Asia, and the Middle East to important cities all around the globe. Uzbekistan Airways, Turkish carriers, Aeroflot, Emirates, and Lufthansa are a few carriers that fly often to Uzbekistan.

2. By Land: If you're coming from one of the nearby nations, you may want to think about entering Uzbekistan through land. Tajikistan, Afghanistan, Turkmenistan, Kazakhstan, Kyrgyzstan, and Uzbekistan are all neighbors of Uzbekistan. Land entrance is possible at border checkpoints and road crossings. However, it's crucial to confirm the border rules and visa requirements in advance since they might change based on your nationality and the particular border crossing you want to utilize.

3. By Train: Uzbekistan has good rail connections to its surrounding nations and beyond. From places such as Moscow, Beijing, Almaty, and Dushanbe among others, there are rail services available. The trains provide relaxing and beautiful rides that let you take in the scenery and stop at different Uzbek locations.

4. By Bus: Taking the bus is an additional alternative, particularly for tourists from neighboring nations.

Buses link Uzbekistan with surrounding countries including Tajikistan, Kazakhstan, and Kyrgyzstan. Bus services are a more cost-effective option for travel, but it's important to familiarize yourself with the routes, timetables, and border-crossing processes before you go.

Depending on your interests and where you want to go in Uzbekistan when you arrive, you may get about utilizing a mix of domestic aircraft, trains, buses, and private or shared taxis.

Before you go on your trip, be sure to verify the necessary visas, any travel warnings, and any entrance limitations imposed by COVID-19. For the most recent and correct information on entrance requirements and travel recommendations, it is advised that you contact the Uzbekistan embassy or consulate in your home country.

Visa Requirements

The kind of visa you need for Uzbekistan depends on your country of citizenship. The following general information about Uzbekistan's visa requirements is provided:

1. Visa Exemption: For a limited time, citizens of a select group of countries may enter Uzbekistan without a visa. For a maximum of 30 days, nationals of Malaysia, Japan, South Korea, Singapore, Israel, and a few more nations can travel to Uzbekistan without a visa. It is essential to confirm the most recent information before your travel since the period of visa-free stays and the countries that qualify may vary.

2. E-Visa: Uzbekistan has an electronic visa (e-visa) system that enables visitors from qualified nations to apply for a visa online in advance of their journey. A single-entry visa with a 30-day maximum stay is available as an e-visa. The application procedure is simple, and the visa is often completed in a short period. It's crucial to submit your e-visa application well in advance of the dates you want to travel.

3. Tourist Visa: You must apply for a tourist visa via the Uzbekistan embassy or consulate in your home country if you are not qualified for a visa exemption or an electronic visa. Depending on your nationality, the criteria may change, but generally speaking, you must submit a completed visa application form, a passport that is currently valid for at least six months, passport-size photos, documentation of your trip plans (such as tickets for a flight or a hotel reservation), and the visa cost. You can also be asked to provide other paperwork, such as a letter of invitation from an Uzbek travel agency.

It's crucial to keep in mind that visa regulations and requirements can change, so it's advised to check the official website of the Uzbek Ministry of Foreign Affairs or contact the closest Uzbek embassy or consulate in your country for the most recent and accurate information regarding visa requirements and application procedures.

Additionally, there can be entrance requirements and limitations on travel during the COVID-19 epidemic. It's important to be aware of any special health or travel warnings about Uzbekistan and to adhere to any instructions given by regional authorities.

The Best Time to Visit and How Long to Stay

Your interests and the experiences you're looking for will play a big role in determining the ideal time to visit Uzbekistan. Nevertheless, the nation typically has a continental climate with scorching summers and chilly winters. Here are some things to think about while visiting Uzbekistan and how long you should stay:

The ideal periods to visit Uzbekistan are usually thought to be in the *spring (April to June)* and fall (September to October). It's the perfect time of year to visit historical places and engage in outdoor activities thanks to the beautiful weather and warm temperatures. The scenery comes to life in the spring with blossoming flowers and lush vegetation, which makes it extremely stunning. Autumn provides pleasant weather with the extra benefit of vibrant foliage.

Summer (July to August): The summer season in Uzbekistan may be hot, with highs as high as 40°C (104°F), especially in the desert areas. But summer might still be a good season to go if you can stand the heat. Just make sure you're dressed appropriately for the weather and that you have sun protection. In addition, Uzbekistan hosts several cultural festivals and events throughout the summer, giving visitors the chance to see local festivities.

Winter (December to February): Uzbekistan's winters may be chilly, particularly in the country's northern and mountainous parts, where lows around zero are not uncommon. However, going during this period may be appropriate for you if you like winter sports like skiing or if you want less traffic and cheaper lodging.

It is advised to remain in Uzbekistan for at least 7 to 10 days to completely take in the country's historical landmarks, cultural experiences, and varied landscapes. With this amount of time, it is possible to thoroughly see important cities like Tashkent, Samarkand, Bukhara, and Khiva while also taking a few side trips to unexplored or less well-known locations.

If you have more time, you may choose to prolong your stay to two weeks or more to allow for a more leisurely exploration and the chance to go to other places or take part in activities like hiking, village visits, or going to local festivals.

The ideal time to go and the amount of time you should spend in Uzbekistan ultimately rely on your tastes, your schedule, and the exact experiences you want to enjoy. It's a good idea to plan your vacation well in advance, taking into account the weather, festival dates, and the activities that you are most interested in.

Choosing Your Destination

It's crucial to take your preferences into account while selecting Uzbekistan travel spots given the variety of options available there. When choosing your travel locations, keep the following things in mind:

- **Wonders of History and Architecture:** Uzbekistan is well known for its ancient cities, each of which has a distinct charm. The three cities of Samarkand, Bukhara, and Khiva, which include magnificent mosques, mausoleums, and madrasas with beautiful tile work, are the architectural jewels of Uzbekistan. These cities, which are UNESCO World Heritage Sites, provide visitors with a look at the lengthy history of the nation. To fully experience its magnificence, think about including these recognizable places on your itinerary.

- **Cultural Immersion:** There are many options to do so in Uzbekistan. Local bazaars like the Chorsu Bazaar in Tashkent or the Siab Bazaar in Samarkand are great places to enjoy the lively atmosphere, try local food, and mingle with welcoming people. Learn more about Uzbek culture by investigating traditional skills like silk weaving in Margilan or pottery craftsmanship in Rishtan. To make your trip more memorable, look for locations that provide genuine cultural experiences.

- **Natural Sceneries:** Uzbekistan's natural splendor goes beyond its ancient monuments. Think about including locations that highlight the nation's varied landscapes. With its enormous dunes and distinctive flora and fauna, the Kyzylkum Desert provides an opportunity to feel the serenity of the desert. The Fergana Valley offers a chance to see traditional agriculture and handicrafts thanks to its lush fields and lovely surroundings. Consider visiting places like the Nuratau-Kyzylkum Biosphere Reserve or the Chatkal Mountains for hiking, animal viewing, or ecotourism if you prefer outdoor activities.

- **Off-the-Beaten-Path:**
  Uzbekistan offers undiscovered treasures just waiting to be discovered, despite the popularity of its main cities as travel destinations. Take into account visiting lesser-known locations

like Shakhrisabz, Tamerlane's birthplace, which is home to stunning architecture and historical value. The southern city of Termez provides a unique fusion of historic Buddhist temples and Islamic buildings. Traveling to these off-the-beaten-path locations may provide a more personal and genuine experience.

• **Personal Interests:** When choosing a place in Uzbekistan, take into account your interests and pastimes. Cities like Bukhara and Samarkand provide fantastic picture possibilities if photography is your passion. Foodies may sample the regional food, visit authentic Uzbek eateries, and take culinary workshops. Visit the Margilan Silk Factory or the Savitsky Museum in Nukus, which holds a great collection of avant-garde art, if you have an interest in textiles.

- **Transportation and Accessibility**: Take into account the practicalities of getting from one place to another. There are several ways to go across Uzbekistan, including domestic aircraft, railroads, and buses. To guarantee a smooth and effective trip, take into account travel times and distances while organizing your schedule.

To make your vacation to Uzbekistan well-rounded and unforgettable, balance your schedule with a variety of historical places, cultural activities, natural landscapes, and personal interests.

Planning Your Trip's Budget

Setting a budget for your trip to Uzbekistan is a crucial part of the preparation for a relaxing and pleasurable visit. When planning your travel budget for Uzbekistan, keep the following in mind:

- **Accommodation:** Depending on the kind of accommodations you choose, the cost of staying in Uzbekistan might change. Guesthouses, hostels, and homestays are affordable choices that might cost anywhere from $15 and $40 per night. Luxury hotels may cost more than $100 per night, while mid-range hotels often cost between $40 and $100 per night. Depending on the location, the degree of comfort, and the facilities offered, prices may change.

- Budgeting for domestic travel inside Uzbekistan should take transportation expenses into account. Domestic flights between major cities are accessible and may range in price from $50 to $150 for a one-way journey, depending on the distance. Ticket costs for trains range from $10 to $30, depending on the type of service and distance, making it a popular and typically more inexpensive choice. For shorter distances, local buses and shared cabs are more affordable choices, usually costing a few dollars.

- **Food and Drinks:** You may discover a variety of eating alternatives to fit your budget in Uzbek cuisine, which is wonderful and diversified. Local eateries and food stand to sell meals for as little as $5, while mid-range restaurants may bill between $10 and $20 a meal. The price of a dinner at a fine restaurant or with an international menu might reach $30 or more. A cost-effective approach to appreciating the gastronomic wonders of Uzbekistan is to sample native street cuisine.

- **Sightseeing and Activities:** Uzbekistan is home to many historical and cultural landmarks, so be sure to include admission costs in your spending plan. Major attractions and museums often charge $3 to $10 per person for admission. Guided tours may incur additional costs; their cost will depend on their length and degree of competence. It's a good idea to set aside some money in your budget for cultural activities like seeing traditional dance or music performances.

- Visa fees, travel insurance, souvenirs, and personal expenditures are other incidental costs to take into account. Your nationality and the kind of visa you need will determine the visa charge. To protect against any unexpected scenarios and medical crises, travel insurance is advised. Prices for souvenirs might vary, although haggling is usual at neighborhood markets. Your vacation will be more flexible if you set aside some money for personal costs like shopping or extra activities.

- The Uzbekistani som (UZS) is the country of Uzbekistan's official currency. It's a good idea to convert your money to some when you arrive in Uzbekistan. Banks, authorized exchange offices, and airports all provide currency exchange services. Although some businesses, especially in bigger cities, take credit cards, it's always a good idea to have some cash on hand for smaller shops and businesses that may not.

Consider any extra charges that are particular to your tastes, such as spa services, nightlife, or certain trips or activities that you are interested in. You'll be able to control your spending and maximize the value of your vacation to Uzbekistan if you have a well-planned budget.

III. TOP 8 MUST-VISIT DESTINATIONS IN UZBEKISTAN

1. Tashkent

The capital of Uzbekistan, Tashkent, is a dynamic metropolis that skillfully combines traditional ways of life with innovations. Here are a few of Tashkent's most popular sights and highlights:

- The spiritual center of Tashkent is **Khast-Imam Square,** which is home to several important structures, including the Tillya Sheikh Mosque, the Barak-Khan Madrasah, and the Islamic Institute of Imam al-Bukhari. One of the earliest copies of the Quran, the legendary Caliph Uthman's Quran, is also found there.

- **Chorsu Bazaar:** With its brilliant displays of fruits, vegetables, spices, meats, and traditional crafts, this crowded and colorful market gives a sensory feast. It's a terrific location to see the local culture firsthand, sample authentic Uzbek food, and go souvenir shopping.

- **Amir Timur Square** is a memorial to the renowned Uzbek conqueror Amir Timur (Tamerlane) and is situated in the center of the city. It has a sizable monument of Amir Timur on a horse, and it is surrounded by lovely fountains and greenery. Both residents and tourists enjoy congregating in the plaza.

- The Senate, the Parliament, and the Presidential Palace are all located in the freedom area, a large area that serves as a symbol of Uzbekistan's freedom. The Independence Monument, a towering column topped with a golden statue emblematic of independence, serves as the focal point of the area.

- This museum, which is housed in the former home of Russian envoy Alexander Polovtsev, offers a thorough picture of the illustrious history and culture of Uzbekistan. It has a wide range of artifacts, archeological discoveries, and displays that highlight the history of the nation.

- **Tashkent Metro:** The Tashkent Metro is not just a mode of transit, but also a tourism experience, thanks to its beautiful architecture and elaborate stations. Beautiful mosaics, chandeliers, and marble accents are used in each station's distinctive design and aesthetic aspects.

- The Alisher Navoi Opera and Ballet Theatre is a magnificent venue that presents opera, ballet, and musical productions. It is a cultural treasure of Tashkent. For lovers of art and culture, it is a must-visit because of its magnificent architecture and opulent interiors.

In addition to these points of interest, Tashkent has a large number of parks, art galleries, retail establishments, and dining establishments where you may take in the energetic atmosphere of the city. You may get a fascinating look at Uzbekistan's history and present by exploring the city's mix of contemporary constructions and ancient sites.

2. Samarkand

Samarkand, a city rich in history, opulence, and architectural wonders, is situated in the center of the Silk Road. Here are a few of Samarkand's most popular sights and highlights:

- **Registan Square** is the heart of Samarkand and one of the most recognizable structures in all of Central Asia. Ulugh Beg Madrasa, Sher-Dor Madrasa, and Tilya-Kori Madrasa are three major madrasas (Islamic schools) that together form a stunning ensemble. It is a beautiful sight, with its delicate tile work, towering arches, and intimidating façade.

- **Gur-e-Amir Mausoleum:** Timur (Tamerlane), a legendary conquistador who made Samarkand his capital, is buried here. It is renowned for its magnificent blue dome, deft mosaic art, and elaborate interiors. Other family members of Timur are also buried at the mausoleum.

- **Necropolis of Shah-i-Zinda:** Shah-i-Zinda is a sacred location with a distinctive array of mausoleums and tombs. Each building in the complex is decorated with elaborate tile work, which results in a captivating display of colors and patterns as it extends down a short, meandering road.

- **Bibi-Khanym Mosque:** Bibi-Khanym Mosque was once one of the biggest and most opulent mosques in the Islamic world. It was constructed by Timur in the 15th century. Its enormous size and traces of the former grandeur, notwithstanding some ruins, make it a striking site to witness.

- **Ulugh Beg Observatory** was one of the most sophisticated astronomical facilities of its day and was built by the famed astronomer and monarch Ulugh Beg. Even though just a small portion of the original construction is still there, it sheds light on the period's scientific advancements.

- **Siab Bazaar** is a lively market where residents congregate to purchase and sell a variety of things, including fresh food, spices, textiles, and traditional crafts. Here, you can immerse yourself in the vivid local culture. It's a fantastic location to take in Samarkand's sights, sounds, and tastes.

- The Afrosiab Museum, which is situated on the ruins of the ancient city of Afrosiab, presents the extensive history of Samarkand and the surrounding area. It has a variety of objects that provide a window into the city's history, such as pottery, frescoes, and antiquated antiques.

For history aficionados, art lovers, and anybody interested in learning more about the glories of the Silk Road, Samarkand is a must-visit destination because of its rich history, architectural treasures, and cultural legacy.

3. Bukhara

The almost 2,000-year-old city of Bukhara is home to a wealth of architectural marvels and serves as a living reminder of the Silk Road period. The following are some of Bukhara's most popular sights and highlights:

- **The Ark of Bukhara:** For centuries, Bukhara's kings lived in this enormous stronghold. You may tour several structures within its walls, such as mosques, royal reception rooms, and a museum that provides details on the city's past.

- **The Kalon Complex,** which dominates the skyline of Bukhara, is made up of the Kalon Minaret, Kalon Mosque, and Miri-Arab Madrasa. An architectural marvel, the 47-meter-tall Kalon Minaret also has exquisite tile work and elaborate motifs, as do the adjoining mosque and madrasa.

- **Samanid Mausoleum:** The Samanid Mausoleum, one of the earliest Central Asian architectural monuments still standing, is a tribute to the expert workmanship of the ninth and tenth centuries. It is a notable cultural and architectural monument because of its simple but attractive brickwork and geometric motifs.

- **The Kalyan Minaret,** popularly known as the Tower of Death, is the focal point of the Po-i-Kalyan Complex. Its 47-meter height has made it a recognizable emblem of Bukhara. The ensemble is completed by the nearby Kalyan Mosque and Miri-Arab Madrasa, both of which include elaborate tile work and decorations.

- The Lyab-i-Hauz Complex is a quiet haven in the middle of the city, built around a large pond. It has the Kukeldash Madrasah and Nodir Devonbegi Madrasa, which together provide a beautiful location for unwinding and taking pleasure in conventional tea shops.

- **Chor Minor:** The Four Minarets, a unique and endearing building, is an architectural wonder. It is a well-liked location for photography because of its four blue-domed minarets and elaborate embellishments, which create a unique picture.

- **Jewish Quarter and Synagogue:** Bukhara has a vibrant Jewish legacy, and visiting the Jewish Quarter will offer you an understanding of the culture and customs of the neighborhood. One of Central Asia's oldest synagogues and a prominent place of worship is the Bukhara Synagogue.

- The UNESCO-listed old town of Bukhara is a well-preserved gem, and exploring its winding lanes and stately buildings is like traveling back in time. The city is a must-visit location for anyone looking for a genuine look into Uzbekistan's illustrious past due to its architectural splendors, cultural legacy, and welcoming friendliness.

4. Khiva

- Khiva is a unique city in Uzbekistan and a UNESCO World Heritage Site. With its intact antique architecture and traditional ambiance, Khiva takes tourists back in time. Here are some of Khiva's most popular sights and highlights:

- The center of Khiva and a living museum in its own right is the ancient walled city of Itchan Kala. Explore its winding lanes, which are dotted with beautiful palaces, mosques, madrasas, and mausoleums, after entering its imposing gates. Itchan Kala provides a window into the illustrious past and architectural wonders of the city.

- The famous **Kalta Minor Minaret,** with its vivid blue tiles and incomplete stature, serves as a representation of Khiva. Although it wasn't built to be the highest minaret in Central Asia, it is nonetheless a striking building that gives the city's skyline individuality.

- **The Kunya-Ark Citadel** was an old fort that housed the Khiva Khans for many years. You may visit several buildings within its borders, including the receiving hall for the Khan, mosques, and the Juma Mosque, which has 218 ornately carved wooden columns.

- **Juma Mosque:** The Juma Mosque is a magnificent architectural marvel noted for its impressive group of wooden columns, each of which has been meticulously carved with a distinctive pattern. It is possible to experience the spiritual and cultural importance of this holy site by going to the mosque during prayer.

- **Tash-Hauli Palace:** With its elaborate gardens, gorgeous tilework, and detailed sculptures, this enormous palace offers an insight into the rich way of life of the Khiva Khans. Explore the harem, reception areas, and summer mosque, among other rooms and halls, in this building.

- **Islam Khodja Minaret and Madrasa:** From its observation deck, the 57-meter-tall Islam

Khodja Minaret provides a bird's-eye view of Khiva. The Islam Khodja Madrasa, which formerly housed a museum displaying traditional crafts and relics, is located next to the minaret.

- **Workshops of the past:** Khiva is renowned for its old-world factories. Discover the city's vibrant marketplaces and artisan studios to see how beautiful fabrics, ceramics, carpets, and woodwork are made. By attending classes and seeing demonstrations, you may even try your hand at traditional crafts.

Khiva is a riveting destination for history buffs, lovers of architecture, and those interested in learning more about Uzbekistan's rich cultural legacy because of its well-preserved ancient town and lovely ambiance. You will have lifelong memories of this dynamic open-air museum after exploring the city's ornate architecture, meandering through its winding alleyways, and taking in Itchan Kala's timeless atmosphere.

5. Shakhrisabz

Amir Timur (Tamerlane), a famous conqueror and politician, was born in Shakhrisabz, sometimes referred to as "Green City," a historic city in Uzbekistan. It combines amazing architectural feats with a storied past and breathtaking scenery. Here are some of Shakhrisabz's best sights and highlights:

- **The Ak-Saray Palace**, often known as the "White Palace," is a striking building that was designed to be among the most opulent palaces of its day. Despite being incomplete, its enormous scale, elaborate tile work, and towering arches provide a look into the Timurid era's exceptional architectural talent.

- **The tomb of Amir Timur** and his immediate family is located in the Dorus-Saodat Complex. The tomb is a magnificent example of Timurid construction and is decorated with beautiful tile work and calligraphy. The Kok Gumbaz Mosque and the last resting place of Timur's spiritual adviser are also part of the complex.

- **Dorut-Tillavat Ensemble:** This religious complex has the Sheikh Shamsuddin Kulyal Mausoleum and the Gumbaz-Seiden Mosque. The tomb is a famous pilgrimage place, and the mosque's blue dome and elaborate façade are stunning architectural features.

- **The Kok Gumbaz Mosque,** which is a part of the

Dorus-Saodat Complex, is distinguished by a large blue dome and exquisite tile work. Visitors may have a unique experience thanks to its exceptional acoustics.

- **Timur's Summer Palace:** Timur's favorite summer hideaway, this lovely compound is situated in the hills around Shakhrisabz. It consists of the grand Chor Minor Pavilion, the actual summer palace, and exquisitely designed gardens.
- **Jehangir's Tomb:** The tomb of Jehangir, Timur's oldest and most beloved son, is a marvel of architecture. It is a great place to visit because of the beautiful mosaic work, calligraphy, and geometric designs.

- **Bazaar and Old Town:** Discover the lively bazaars and quaint alleys of the old town to fully immerse yourself in the local culture. Here, you may sample authentic Uzbek cuisine, browse for local products, and take in the lively pace of daily life.

History buffs and those looking for a distinctive look into Uzbekistan's past will find Shakhrisabz to be a fascinating trip because of its historical importance, impressive architectural legacy, and beautiful natural settings. You will be transported to a bygone age of grandeur and cultural magnificence by exploring the city's majestic architecture, wandering through its historic streets, and learning the history behind each monument.

6. Termez

The historic city of Termez, which is situated in southern Uzbekistan close to the Afghan border, has a long history dating back more than 2,500 years. It is renowned for its historical landmarks, religious structures, and archaeological sites. Here are some of Termez's main landmarks and attractions:

- **Fayaz Tepe:** Take a tour of the 2nd century BC archeological site at Fayaz Tepe. It includes stupas, elaborate paintings, and the remnants of Buddhist monasteries that provide light on the area's former Buddhist culture.

- **Sultan Saodat Ensemble:** This complex, which is regarded as a prominent pilgrimage destination, houses the graves of several famous Sufi sheiks. It is a calm location to visit because of its magnificent architecture, dexterous tile work, and peaceful environment.

- Visit the historic Kirk Kiz fortification, which translates to

"Fortress of Forty Girls," which is surrounded by legends and has sweeping views of the region.

- Explore Termez's past in the Archaeological Museum, which has a remarkable collection of items, including Buddhist relics, Islamic artwork, and regional archaeological discoveries.

- Visit the tomb of renowned Islamic scholar Al-Hakim At-Termizi at the Al-Hakim At-Termizi Mausoleum. The turquoise dome and exquisite construction of the tomb make it a significant religious and historical attraction.

- Discover the extensive Termez archaeological zone, which includes several historic remains and structures. Learn about the history of the city by exploring the ruins of old forts, Buddhist temples, and archaeological riches.

- Termez and Afghanistan are connected by the Friendship Bridge, which you may drive or walk over. Witness the busy economic and cultural exchanges that take place at this international border crossing while taking in the beautiful vistas of the Amu Darya River.

A greater appreciation of Uzbekistan's rich history may be gained by visiting Termez, which provides a unique fusion of historical places, spiritual locations, and cultural experiences. For those looking for an excursion off the usual route, its ancient marvels, religious structures, and closeness to the border make it an alluring location.

7. The Fergana Valley

The Fergana Valley is a beautiful and productive area in eastern Uzbekistan that also includes a small portion of Tajikistan and Kyrgyzstan. It is renowned for its breathtaking scenery, artisanal craftsmanship, and extensive cultural legacy. Here are some of the Fergana Valley's features and attractions:

- **Visit Margilan,** a medieval city renowned for producing silk. Investigate the Yodgorlik Silk Factory to see how silk is traditionally produced, from spinning the cocoons to weaving fine garments. You may get premium silk items in the Margilan Silk Factory Market, so don't miss it.

- **Rishton:** Explore the pottery town known for its vibrantly colored, hand-painted ceramics. Explore the studios to see how pottery is made and how it has been handed down through the years. Beautifully produced pottery is available to purchase as gifts or home décor.

- **Kokand:** Take a tour of this once-important Silk Road trade center. Visit the Khudayar Khan Palace, a masterpiece of architecture with exquisite wood carvings, mosaics, and courtyards. For their distinctive architectural designs, the Jami Mosque and the Norbut-Biy Madrasa are also worthwhile visits.

- Find out more about Babur, the man who founded the Mughal Empire in India, in the city of Andijan. Visit the Babur Museum to see items from Babur's life and the local area's cultural history.

Additionally, Andijan has a bustling market where you may browse local wares and take in the culture.

- **Fergana:** Visit the vibrant city of Fergana, which serves as the Fergana Valley's administrative hub. Discover the Kumtepa Bazaar, a bustling marketplace where you can buy a variety of products such as clothing, crafts, and fresh food. For further information on the history and culture of the area, you can also pay a visit to the Fergana Regional Museum.

- **Landscapes & Mountains:** The Fergana Valley is encircled by stunning mountain ranges that provide chances for trekking, nature drives, and hikes. Outdoor enthusiasts often go to the Chatkal Range and the Alay Mountains because of the breathtaking vistas they provide.

- **Cultural Experiences:** Get a true sense of the community by taking part in craft classes, visiting local artists, or seeing traditional music and dance performances. As a result of the Fergana Valley's well-known rich cultural legacy, participating in the local customs gives your trip a special touch.

For those looking for a genuine cultural experience, the Fergana Valley is a mesmerizing destination because of its stunning natural surroundings, traditional crafts, and friendly people. You will have long-lasting recollections of this vivacious and scenic location after seeing the valley's towns, interacting with local craftspeople, and taking in the breathtaking scenery.

8. Nuratau Mountains

The beautiful Nuratau Mountains, which divide the Navoi and Samarkand districts of Uzbekistan, are situated in the country's center. This mountain range provides chances for outdoor sports, spectacular natural beauty, and a variety of flora and wildlife. Here are a few of the Nuratau Mountains' best features and attractions:

- Discover the Chimgan Mountains, a well-liked location within the Nuratau range. Take in the breathtaking scenery, alpine meadows, and pristine lakes. The area is perfect for mountain biking, hiking, and trekking since there are paths for all skill levels.

- Visit the Charvak Reservoir, a charming lake tucked away in the Nuratau Mountains. The calm environment of the turquoise seas and lush green hills are ideal for swimming, picnics, and water activities like jet skiing and boating.

- **Village of Hayat:** Discover the traditional village lifestyle in Hayat, which is situated in the Nuratau Mountains' foothills. Engage in conversation with the welcoming inhabitants, discover their customs and traditions, and see examples of regional handicrafts including pottery and carpet weaving.

- Discover the protected region known as the Nuratau-Kyzylkum Biosphere Reserve, which includes a portion of the Nuratau Mountains and the enormous Kyzylkum Desert. Numerous plant and animal species, including rare and imperiled ones like Severtsov's sheep and Bukhara deer, may be found in this complex habitat.

- Explore the Sarmyshsay Rock Art Gallery, which is situated in the Nuratau Mountains' foothills. Ancient rock carvings and petroglyphs from thousands of years ago that portray scenes from ancient civilizations' everyday life and hunting are on display in this outdoor museum.

- **Nurata:** Travel to this town, which is located at the base of the Nuratau Mountains. Discover its historical landmarks, including the Nuratau-Kyzylkum Biosphere Reserve Visitor Center, the antiquated Nur Fortress, and the treasured Chashma Spring by Zoroastrians and Muslims alike.

- **Birdwatching:** Avid birdwatchers will find plenty of possibilities in the Nuratau Mountains. You may see a wide range of bird species there, including eagles, vultures, hoopoes, and warblers, thanks to its different habitats.

VI. 6 ANCIENT HISTORY AND CULTURE TO SEE

1. UNESCO World Heritage Sites

Several UNESCO World Heritage Sites can be found in Uzbekistan, which highlights the value of the nation's rich cultural and historical heritage. Here are a few of Uzbekistan's noteworthy UNESCO World Heritage Sites:

- Bukhara's historical core is a well-preserved illustration of a former Silk Road commercial hub. It includes a variety of magnificent architectural structures, including mosques, madrasas, mausoleums, and minarets. The layout and architecture of the city show the impact of the many Silk Road civilizations.

- Amir Timur (Tamerlane) was born at Shakhrisyabz, which is a remarkable location that displays the magnificence of Timurid architecture. It has famous buildings including the Kok Gumbaz Mosque, the Dorus-Saodat Complex, and the Ak-Saray Palace.

- Samarkand, one of the oldest towns still under continuous human habitation in Central Asia, is well known for its stunning Islamic architecture. The city's well-known features include Registan Square, the Gur-e-Amir Mausoleum, the Bibi-Khanym Mosque, and the Shah-i-Zinda necropolis.

- Khiva's medieval inner city, Itchan Kala, is distinguished for its mud-brick walls and maintained historical architecture. The location is home to a large number of palaces, mosques, madrasas, and mausoleums that illustrate Khiva's importance as a Silk Road commercial hub.

- The Old Town in Tashkent, which is located in the old city of Tashkent, is a testament to the place's lengthy history. Architectural icons including the Kukeldash Madrasa, Sheikhantaur Ensemble, and Barak-Khan Madrasa are among its highlights.

These Uzbekistan UNESCO World Heritage Sites provide a window into the nation's glorious history by highlighting its magnificent architectural achievements, rich cultural legacy, and importance along the ancient Silk Road. Visitors may get a greater understanding of the many different influences and exceptional workmanship that formed Uzbekistan's history by seeing these locations.

2. Silk Road History

As a prehistoric network of trade routes that linked East and West and allowed for the movement of products, ideas, and cultures across numerous civilizations, the Silk Road is significant historically. Ferdinand von Richthofen, a German geographer, first used the name "Silk Road" to describe these trade routes' profitable silk industry in the 19th century.

The Silk Road, which had its beginnings in China, covered thousands of kilometers, passing through Central Asia, the Middle East, and Europe. Along the route, various things including spices, rare metals, jewels, pottery, and exotic fruits were transported in addition to silk, one of the most valued commodities.

The rise of civilizations along the Silk Road's route was greatly influenced by it. It promoted the dissemination of ideas, ideologies, and information, fostering intercultural dialogue and the growth of cosmopolitan cities.

These pathways allowed for the transmission of Chinese technologies including papermaking, gunpowder, and printing skills as well as Buddhism from India, Islam from the Middle East, and subsequently Christianity from Europe.

Cities along the Silk Road prospered as thriving hubs of trade and cultural interaction. Among the important commerce centers that prospered along the route were Samarkand, Bukhara, Kashgar, Xi'an, and Constantinople (now Istanbul).

These towns evolved into mingling grounds for many customs, languages, and civilizations, leaving behind a spectacular architectural heritage of mosques, palaces, caravanserais, and bazaars.

Due to many circumstances, including the development of marine trade routes and geopolitical shifts, the Silk Road started to deteriorate in the 15th century. The Silk Road's influence, nevertheless, is still felt in the areas it once united.

Many of the Silk Road's towns and archaeological monuments are now listed as UNESCO World Heritage monuments, drawing both visitors and academics interested in learning more about this unique period of human history.

The Silk Road is still a potent representation of commerce, cross-cultural ties, and the tenacity of human inventiveness. Its legacy encourages understanding and respect for the many civilizations that formed the world we live in today by serving as a reminder of the strength of interchange and interaction

3. Museums and Art Galleries

The museums and art galleries in Uzbekistan provide intriguing insights into the nation's history, culture, and customs. Here are some noteworthy Uzbek museums and galleries to visit:

- **The State Museum of Uzbekistan's** History is a museum in Tashkent that displays Uzbekistan's history from antiquity to the present. It has a large collection of antiquities, which includes historical records, historical papers, traditional clothing, and works of art.

- The Amir Timur Museum in Tashkent has relics from Amir Timur's (Tamerlane's) rule, including weaponry, manuscripts, jewelry, and miniature paintings. The museum is devoted to preserving Amir Timur's (Tamerlane's) history. The museum provides details on the life and accomplishments of this illustrious conqueror of Central Asia.

- **Uzbekistan's State Museum of Arts (Tashkent):** This museum is home to a sizable collection of the country's priceless works of art. Artworks from the past and the present are on display, including complex woodcarvings, paintings, sculptures, fabrics, and ceramics. Additionally, the museum sponsors cultural activities and transient exhibits.

- **The Navoi State Museum** of Literature is located in Tashkent and celebrates the literary legacy of Uzbekistan by paying tribute to its most renowned poets, authors, and thinkers. It offers an insight into Uzbekistan's illustrious literary heritage by displaying manuscripts, books, and personal items of notable authors.

- **The Museum of Applied Arts in Tashkent** displays a wide variety of Uzbek applied arts and crafts in a stunning home from the late 19th century. Visitors may enjoy the fine woodwork, textiles, jewelry, and pottery produced in the area using traditional methods and skilled workmanship.

- **State Museum of Art (Samarkand):** This Samarkand museum has an exceptional collection of ancient artwork, including statues, frescoes, and ceramics from the long history of the area. The museum's features include artwork from the Timurid Empire and antiquities from the ancient city of Afrasiab.

- **The Museum of Savitsky Art Collection (Nukus)** is home to a remarkable collection of Russian avant-garde artwork and folk art from Karakalpakstan. Nukus is the nation's capital. It contains pieces created by well-known artists like Igor Savitsky, who devoted his life to safeguarding and advancing these distinctive aesthetic traditions.

It is possible to get a greater knowledge of Uzbekistan's cultural heritage, creative accomplishments, and historical contributions by visiting these museums and art galleries. For art lovers and history buffs alike, Uzbekistan's museums provide a wealth of information and enthralling experiences, regardless of your interest in archaeology, literature, traditional crafts, or contemporary art.

5. Traditional Crafts and Markets

Uzbekistan has a long history of workmanship, and its marketplaces are thriving centers for the revival of old crafts. It's fun to explore the traditional markets and crafts in Uzbekistan because you can see the talent and imagination of the country's craftspeople. You may find the following traditional crafts and markets:

- **Silk Weaving:** Silk weaving is a traditional skill that has been carried out for many years in Uzbekistan, which is known for its silk output. Visit the Yodgorlik Silk Factory in Margilan, a region known for producing silk, where you can see the delicate process of silk weaving in progress and buy high-quality silk goods.
- **Pottery & Ceramics:** Rishton is renowned for its vivid, hand-painted pottery. Visit the Rishton studios to see how pottery is made, from sculpting the clay to painting elaborate patterns. Beautifully made ceramic dishes, bowls, and ornamental objects are available for purchase.

- **Textiles and carpets:** Uzbekistan is well known for its magnificent textiles and carpets. Investigate the marketplaces in towns like Bukhara and Samarkand where you may discover a variety of handmade carpets, embroidered clothing, suzani wall hangings, and conventional ikat fabrics.

- **Woodcarving:** Intricately carved wooden furniture, doors, and columns are common examples of this ancient skill in Uzbekistan. Visit the stores in towns like Khiva and Bukhara to see the mastery of the carvers and discover one-of-a-kind wooden products.

- **Metalworking:** Uzbekistani craftsmen have a long tradition of producing exquisite brass and copper objects. Find handmade metal items including trays, teapots, and jewelry in the marketplaces of Tashkent and Bukhara.

- **Jewelry:** Uzbekistan is renowned for its elaborate patterns and use of precious and semi-precious gemstones in its traditional jewelry production. Silver necklaces, bracelets, earrings, and rings are among the exquisite items you may purchase at the jewelry markets in Samarkand and Bukhara.

- **Traditional marketplaces (Bazaars):** Uzbekistan's traditional marketplaces, sometimes referred to as bazaars, are lively locales where you may get a feel for the community. Discover the Chorsu Bazaar, Siab Bazaar, and Lyab-i Hauz Complex in Tashkent, Samarkand, and Bukhara, where you can buy a wide range of products, including fresh food, spices, dried fruits, fabrics, and handicrafts.

You may see the skills and methods handed down through the centuries and purchase one-of-a-kind, handmade gifts that showcase the rich cultural history of Uzbekistan by visiting these traditional craft studios and fairs. It's a great chance to help out local craftspeople and take some of Uzbekistan's customary workmanship home with you.

Local Events and Festivals

Uzbekistan is a nation that enjoys year-round festivals and events to honor its rich culture and customs. These celebrations provide a special chance to get acquainted with the regional traditions, music, dancing, and food. The following are some of the major holidays and occasions that are observed in Uzbekistan:

The traditional Persian New Year is called Navruz, and it is celebrated widely in Uzbekistan on March 21. It heralds the start of spring and is a season of celebration and rejuvenation. People congregate to take part in music and dancing performances and to consume traditional foods like sumalak, a unique wheat meal made for Navruz.

The Silk and Spice Festival, which takes place in the historic city of Bukhara in May or June, honors the area's long history of commerce. The event offers visitors an opportunity to explore the rich culture and history of the Silk Road by showcasing ancient crafts including silk weaving, carpet making, pottery making, and spice trade.

August brings about the annual Sharq Taronalari (Melodies of the East) International Music Festival, which brings together artists from all over the globe to honor the many musical traditions of other nations. Visitors may take in concerts, performances, and contests that include both local and foreign musical styles.

In September, the hamlet of Sentob, close to Samarkand, hosts the Asrlar Sadosi (Echo of Centuries) Festival. The preservation and promotion of Uzbekistan's traditional arts, crafts, and cultural heritage are its main objectives.

Visitors may take part in workshops, see traditional performances, and view displays showcasing diverse traditional crafts and traditions.

Kokand, a city renowned for its long history of silk manufacturing and handicrafts, holds the annual Qoqon Silk and Handicraft Festival in October. It displays the traditional arts and crafts of the area, such as silk weaving, embroidery, woodworking, and metalworking. Visitors may take in live concerts, buy genuine handcrafted items, and watch live demonstrations.

The Karshi-Khanabad Crafts Festival honors traditional crafts and is held in the southern Uzbek city of Karshi in October or November. Local craftsmen showcase their abilities in wood carving, needlework, metalwork, and ceramics. Visitors may see the artists at work, talk to them, and buy one-of-a-kind handcrafted keepsakes.

These celebrations and activities provide a superb chance to get a taste of Uzbekistan's rich cultural heritage. They provide a window into the nation's customs, music, dance, crafts, and gastronomic pleasures, producing priceless experiences for both residents and guests. The precise dates and locations of these events should be confirmed since they may change from year to year.

VI. MODERN ADVENTURES IN UZBEKISTAN

Outdoor Activities

For outdoor adventurers and nature lovers, Uzbekistan's various landscapes and natural beauties provide a broad variety of outdoor activities. Here are some thrilling outdoor activities to take part in Uzbekistan, from visiting gorgeous mountains to crossing enormous deserts:

- **Trekking and Hiking:** The Tian Shan and Pamir-Alai mountain ranges, which are found in Uzbekistan, both provide excellent trekking and hiking options. Outdoor enthusiasts often go to the Nuratau-Kyzylkum Biosphere Reserve and the Chimgan Mountains near Tashkent. You may go out on multi-day excursions, investigate picturesque pathways, and take in stunning panoramas all along the way.

- **Camping:** By camping in Uzbekistan, you may get a close-up view of the stunning natural surroundings of the nation. Camping in the Nuratau-Kyzylkum Biosphere Reserve, in the Kyzylkum desert, or next to a lovely alpine lake will all allow you to spend tranquil evenings beneath the stars and awake to breathtaking scenery.

- Uzbekistan is a portion of the enormous Kyzylkum Desert, which provides opportunities for exhilarating desert activities. Discover the distinctive atmosphere of the desert, see stunning sunsets, and go on a camel trip across the dunes. For an adrenaline sensation, you may also try quad biking or sandboarding.

- **Wildlife Watching:** A variety of uncommon and endangered species may be found in Uzbekistan's flora and wildlife. Explore the Chatkal and Zaamin National Parks to see a variety of animals, including birds, deer, ibex, mountain goats, and mountain lions. With so many species to see in their native surroundings, birdwatching is especially well-liked in Uzbekistan.

- **River Rafting and Kayaking:** There are exhilarating options for river rafting and kayaking on the Zarafshan and Surkhandarya Rivers. Navigating through the rapids while being surrounded by beautiful scenery and mountain vistas is a test of your abilities. Trips for rafting and kayaking are offered at several ability levels, making them accessible to both novice and expert paddlers.

- **Skiing and snowboarding:** The Chimgan Mountains near Tashkent became a well-liked location for these winter sports. There are several degrees of difficulty on the slopes, and you may hire equipment there. As you skim down the slopes, take in the refreshing mountain air and breathtaking snowy scenery.

- **Hot Air Ballooning:** Take a hot air balloon flight to see the landscapes of Uzbekistan from a different angle. Admire breathtaking panoramic views as you float over scenic valleys, mountains, and historic towns like Bukhara or Samarkand.

Thrilling experiences may be had when exploring the different landscapes of Uzbekistan thanks to its natural treasures and outdoor pursuits. Uzbekistan has something to offer everyone, whether they choose a stroll, an adrenaline-pumping encounter, or just to lose themselves in the beauty of nature.

Food and Drink Scene

The geographical location of Uzbekistan and historical exchanges along the Silk Road have had an impact on the country's delectable fusion of tastes in the food and beverage industry. Here are some highlights of Uzbek cuisine, which range from flavorful meat meals and cool drinks to fragrant pilaf:

- **Plov (Pilaf):** Plov is a delectable national dish of Uzbekistan. It includes rice, meat—typically lamb or beef—carrots, onions, and an assortment of spices. The meal is carefully cooked in a large kazan (cauldron) to generate rich tastes, and fried onions, raisins, and chickpeas are often added as a garnish.

- **Shashlik:** In Uzbek cuisine, shashlik is a well-known grilled beef dish. Skewered lamb, beef, or chicken pieces are grilled over an open flame to produce soft, tasty meat. It often comes with a side of tart tomato sauce, fresh bread, and thinly sliced onions.

- **Manti:** Manti is steamed dumplings that are stuffed with onions and seasoned meat, usually lamb or beef. They often come with a tomato-based sauce and are topped with a dollop of sour cream. Manti is a tasty starter or main dish that comes in a variety of sizes.

- **Lagman:** Lagman is a thick, hand-made noodle soup cooked with a variety of vegetables, including bell peppers, carrots, and onions, as well as meat (often beef or lamb). It is seasoned with fragrant herbs and spices to produce a meal that is fulfilling and savory.

- **Samsa:** Savory pastry stuffed with minced meat (often lamb), onions, and spices. The dough is cooked until it is golden and crunchy on the outside with a tasty meat filling within. In Uzbekistan, samsa is a well-liked appetizer or snack.

- **Green Tea:** In Uzbek culture, green tea has a particular position and is often offered as a sign of friendliness. Typically, it is served with conventional sweets like halva or dried fruits. The mild and aromatic flavor of Uzbek green tea makes it a delicious drink.

- **Non (Uzbek Bread):** A mainstay of Uzbek cooking is non. This circular, flatbread is freshly made and eaten with virtually every meal. It is often decorated with ornamental designs. The bread is light and fluffy, making it ideal for breaking apart and enjoying different foods.

- **Ayran:** Ayran is a well-known traditional yogurt-based beverage in Uzbekistan. To make it, combine yogurt, water, and a dash of salt. Ayran is a cold and revitalizing beverage, particularly in the sweltering summertime.

Fresh salads, soups, dairy items like kurut (dried yogurt balls), and a selection of pastries and sweets are also available while eating in Uzbekistan. You may savor the bright tastes and discover the genuine taste of Uzbek cuisine, which represents the nation's rich culinary tradition and cultural influences, by exploring the neighborhood food markets and eateries.

Entertainment and Nightlife

The nightlife and entertainment industry in Uzbekistan is thriving, especially in the larger cities like Tashkent and Samarkand. There are still many possibilities for enjoying a night out, even if the nightlife may not be as active as in some other places. Here are some of Uzbekistan's entertainment and nightlife scene's high points:

- **Restaurants and cafes:** Uzbekistan's cities are littered with a variety of eateries that provide a wide range of cuisines as well as live entertainment and music. You may have a delectable lunch while listening to live performances of classic or modern music. Additionally, many places provide outside dining, which creates a wonderful setting for mingling and enjoying the evening.

- **Bars and lounges:** There are an increasing number of bars and lounges in Tashkent, where you may unwind with a drink and mingle with others. These places provide a variety of alcoholic and non-alcoholic drinks, including domestic and foreign options. In addition to hosting DJ sets or live music performances, several establishments also foster a dynamic atmosphere.

- **Theaters and Opera Houses:** Uzbekistan has a long history of performing arts, and seeing a show at one of the nation's famed theaters or opera houses is a must-do cultural experience. The Samarkand State Academic Drama Theatre provides an opportunity to see regional theatrical plays, while the Navoi Opera and Ballet Theatre in Tashkent is famed for its opulent performances.

- **Performances of Traditional Music and Dance:** Traditional music and dance are well-known in Uzbekistan. Traditional Uzbek music, dance, and folklore are often performed in a variety of settings, including cultural institutions and concert halls. These performances are a pleasure for fans of music and dance and provide a window into the nation's cultural history.

- **Street Markets and Night Bazaars:** In certain cities, street markets and night bazaars come alive at night, providing a distinctive shopping and entertainment experience. You may browse these crowded markets, eat some of the local food, look for one-of-a-kind gifts, and take in the vibrant environment.

- **Casinos and Gaming Facilities:** If you're looking for a little excitement, certain hotels in bigger cities may feature casinos or gaming facilities where you may try your luck at slot machines, roulette, or card games. For customers seeking excitement, these places provide a new sort of entertainment.

It's important to keep in mind that Uzbekistan's nightlife environment may vary and is more constrained than in certain other places. Respecting local traditions and laws is also crucial, especially those that deal with alcohol usage and attire. While taking advantage of Uzbekistan's nightlife and entertainment opportunities, it is essential to inquire about any special advice or guidelines and to abide by local customs.

Shopping and Souvenirs

With a vast variety of traditional crafts, fabrics, and mementos that represent the nation's rich cultural past, shopping in Uzbekistan provides a distinctive experience. As you plan your shopping and souvenir purchases, keep the following in mind:

- Uzbekistan is well known for its excellent handwoven textiles, notably its ikat textiles. These fabrics include brilliant colors and detailed designs. In markets and specialist textile stores, you may get ikat scarves, apparel, and home décor items like pillow covers and wall hangings.

- **Pottery & Ceramics:** Uzbek ceramics are renowned for their expert workmanship and elaborate patterns. You may discover a selection of ceramic objects with classic designs and themes, from ornamental plates and bowls to tea sets and vases. Rishtan is well-known for its blue-glazed ceramics.

- **Suzani embroidery** is a traditional embroidery style used in Uzbekistan. These vibrantly embroidered fabrics are often used as pillowcases, bed coverings, and wall hangings. They make for lovely, one-of-a-kind keepsakes that decorate your house with a hint of Uzbek artistry.

- **Handmade Carpets and Rugs**: Uzbekistan is well-known for its handmade carpets and rugs, which use conventional patterns and manufacturing processes. These intricately woven works of art, which display the talent and craftsmanship of regional weavers, come in a variety of shapes and designs. Samarkand and Bukhara are well known for their carpet manufacturing.

- **Miniature Paintings**: Influenced by Central Asian and Persian traditions, miniature paintings are a distinctive style of art in Uzbekistan. These elaborate drawings, which are primarily created on paper or camel bone, often include historical and cultural topics. They create beautiful collections and ornamental objects.

- **Traditional Musical Instruments**: If you like music, you may want to get an authentic Uzbek instrument. Music businesses sell instruments like the doira (frame drum), tambur (long-necked string instrument), and dutar (long-necked lute), which make wonderful mementos for music lovers.

- **Spices & Dry Fruits:** The bright spice markets of Uzbekistan are renowned for their broad selection of fragrant spices, including cumin, coriander, and turmeric. A variety of dried fruits, including figs, raisins, and apricots, are also available. You may enjoy them as delectable snacks while traveling or bring them home.

Don't forget to visit regional marketplaces and bazaars when shopping in Uzbekistan, such as the Chorsu Bazaar in Tashkent or the Siyob Bazaar in Samarkand. In these bustling marketplaces, a variety of things are available, and haggling is usual. Before making purchases, it is usually a good idea to verify customs policies on the import of certain commodities.

Shopping in Uzbekistan enables you to support regional producers, bring home one-of-a-kind keepsakes that are vital to the local culture, and preserve the memories of your trip to this captivating nation.

Shopping Malls

Bazaar Chorsu, Tashkent:

In Tashkent, Uzbekistan, at Navoiy Street

One of Tashkent's oldest and most well-known bazaars is the Chorsu Bazaar. Fresh vegetables, spices, fabrics, handicrafts, and souvenirs are just a few of the many goods it sells. Ceramics, traditional costumes, exquisitely woven fabrics, and other items are available.

Samarkand's Siyob Bazaar:

Address: Samarkand, Uzbekistan, Siyob Street

In the center of Samarkand, there is a lively bazaar called Siyob Bazaar. You may look through a range of products here, including fruits, veggies, handicrafts, and souvenirs. Be on the lookout for Uzbekistan-inspired spices, embroidered linens, silk scarves, and beautiful pottery.

The Bukhara Trading Domes:
In Bukhara, Uzbekistan, at Toqi Sarrafon Street

The Bukhara Bazaar sometimes referred to as the Bukhara Trading Domes, is a famous market center in Bukhara. Numerous stores offering carpets, clothing, jewelry, spices, and traditional crafts are housed in the dome-shaped buildings. It's a fantastic location to discover one-of-a-kind gifts and take in Bukhara's energetic environment.

The Rishtan Ceramics Workshop:
Address: Fergana Valley, Rishtan, Uzbekistan

A trip to Rishtan is essential if you're looking to buy magnificent blue-glazed pottery. You may visit the local potters' studios in this little village in the Fergana Valley and buy genuine pottery straight from the craftspeople. The address could change based on the workshop you go to.

The Samarkand Silk Carpet Factory:
In Samarkand, Uzbekistan, at M39

Samarkand is known for its silk carpets, and a trip to the Samarkand Silk Carpet Factory gives you the chance to see how they are manufactured in an old-fashioned way and buy finely crafted carpets. Depending on the particular carpet manufacturer you visit, the address could change.

Uzbekistan is home to a great number of other marketplaces, stores, and businesses. You'll get the chance to support regional artists and find one-of-a-kind treasures by exploring these places.

VIII. ACCOMODATION OPTIONS

Top Recommended Hotels and Resorts

Located in Tashkent is the Hyatt Regency
Address: 1A Navoi Street, Tashkent, Uzbekistan 100017

The Hyatt Regency in the center of Tashkent provides opulent lodging with contemporary conveniences. The hotel offers opulent accommodations, a variety of eateries and bars, a spa, a fitness center, and an outdoor swimming pool. It is strategically located close to important attractions and commercial areas.

Tashkent's Lotte City Hotel Tashkent Palace:
Address: 56 Navoi Street, Tashkent, Uzbekistan 100017

Lotte City Hotel Tashkent Palace is a stylishly renovated 19th-century structure that combines old-world elegance with modern luxury. The hotel has large rooms, a restaurant on the roof with panoramic views, a fitness facility, and a courtyard garden. It is close to well-known attractions and commercial centers.

Samarkand's Registan Plaza Hotel:
M. Alimova Street, #1, Samarkand, Uzbekistan 140100

Registan Plaza Hotel provides pleasant lodgings with traditional Uzbek design close to the famous Registan Square. The hotel offers several dining choices, including a spa, a rooftop patio, an outdoor pool, and well-appointed rooms. The ancient sites of Samarkand may be easily explored because of their central position.

Bukhara's **Malika Bukhara Hotel:**
Address: 7, Khakikat Street, Bukhara, Uzbekistan 200118

With its classic Uzbek architecture and welcoming service, the Malika Bukhara Hotel, which is situated in the center of Bukhara's Old Town, makes for a pleasant stay. The hotel has a courtyard garden, a restaurant offering Uzbek cuisine, pleasant rooms decorated with regional artwork, and a helpful staff that can provide suggestions for nearby attractions.

Khiva's **Shaherezada Boutique Hotel:**

Pahlavan Mahmud Street, 33, Khiva, Uzbekistan 220900

Shaherezada Boutique Hotel provides a distinctive stay in a UNESCO World Heritage site. It is located within the historic city of Khiva's old walls. The hotel offers convenient access to the city's attractions, cozy rooms adorned with traditional themes, a rooftop terrace with panoramic views, a restaurant offering Uzbek and European cuisine, and more.

Please keep in mind that the addresses given are just for reference, and it is always essential to double-check the precise location and contact information before making bookings. To ensure a pleasant stay in Uzbekistan, these hotels provide a variety of facilities, comfort, and close access to popular activities.

Other Accommodation Options

You may choose from a variety of lodging alternatives in Uzbekistan to fit a variety of budgets and interests. Here are some common lodging options to think about:

- **Hotels:** There are many hotels in Uzbekistan, ranging from opulent five-star establishments to reasonably priced lodgings. Major towns like Tashkent, Samarkand, and Bukhara have a variety of hotels with contemporary amenities including cozy rooms, dining options, spas, and exercise facilities. The presence of global hotel brands like Hyatt, Radisson, and Hilton in Uzbekistan guarantees a high level of comfort and service.

- **Boutique Hotels:** Think about staying at a boutique hotel for a more personalized and distinctive experience. These tiny hotels often have pleasant settings, lovely furnishings, and attentive service. Boutique hotels may be found in both well-known cities and off-the-beaten-track locations, letting you fully experience the local way of life.

- **Guesthouses and Homestays:** Think about staying in a guesthouse or homestay to experience true Uzbek hospitality. These choices provide the chance to stay with local families and get insight into their daily routines. Smaller towns and rural locations often include guesthouses and homestays that provide an opportunity to interact with the local population.

- **Caravanserais:** Renovated caravanserais that were originally used as rest stops for traders on the Silk Road may be seen in certain towns. These old structures have been renovated into interesting lodging alternatives, giving visitors a look at the long history of the nation. A caravanserai stay provides a combination of comfort and heritage.

- **Yurts and Desert Camps:** You may choose to stay in a yurt or a desert camp when visiting Uzbekistan's desert areas, such as the Kyzylkum Desert. These lodging options provide an opportunity to explore the grandeur of the desert area while staying in authentic nomadic-style tents. Yurts and desert camps provide simple comforts and a special connection to nature.

It's a good idea to make your hotel reservations in advance, particularly during busy travel times. When selecting your lodging, take into account the neighborhood, amenities, and reviews.

Uzbekistan provides a variety of accommodations to meet any traveler's requirements, whether you like the convenience of a contemporary hotel or the beauty of a traditional guesthouse.

VII. PRACTICAL INFORMATION AND TIPS

Safety and Health

Prioritizing your health and safety is vital while visiting Uzbekistan. The following advice can help you have a safe and healthy trip:

- Before your journey, review the most recent travel warnings and updates issued by your government or other relevant authorities. These warnings detail any security issues, health dangers, or limitations on travel to Uzbekistan.

- **Purchase travel insurance:** It is strongly advised that you purchase travel insurance that provides coverage for unexpected costs, such as medical bills and trip cancellations. The policy's coverage, including any exclusions or limits, should be reviewed and understood.

- **Consult a Travel Health expert:** Discuss any required immunizations, prescriptions, or health precautions with a healthcare expert or travel health clinic well in advance of your trip. Measles, mumps, rubella, diphtheria, tetanus, and influenza immunizations, among others, should be current.

- **Drink bottled water** and abstain from tap water and beverages with ice from unidentified sources to stay hydrated and consume safe food. Be careful while eating food on the street and choose well-prepared meals from renowned restaurants. Use hand sanitizer as needed or often wash your hands with soap and water.

- Keep your possessions safe and exercise caution in busy locations, especially against theft and pickpocketing. Be careful not to flaunt your affluence or carry a lot of cash. When taking public transportation, choose dependable services and proceed with caution.

- **Respect Local Customs and Laws:** Learn about Uzbekistan's regional laws, traditions, and customs. When attending places of worship, dress modestly. To guarantee a seamless and pleasant trip, abide by local laws and respect cultural sensitivity.

- **Stay Informed:** Keep yourself aware of your surroundings and any hazards. Pay close attention to local news, weather reports, and any cautions or advisories about travel. Upon arrival, register with your embassy or consulate to obtain critical information and help if required.

- **COVID-19 Considerations:** The COVID-19 pandemic is continuing strong as of the knowledge cutoff date of September 2021. Keep up with the most recent COVID-19-related travel regulations, entrance restrictions, and health precautions. Observe suggested rules including donning masks, keeping your distance from others, and often washing your hands.

Keep in mind that it's wise to be cautious and apply common sense while traveling. You may have a pleasant and joyful time discovering the beauties of Uzbekistan if you take the required safety measures and pay attention to your health and well-being.

Banking and Currency

The Uzbekistani som (UZS) is the country of Uzbekistan's official currency. The following are some significant facts concerning money and banking in Uzbekistan:

- **Currency Exchange**: Authorized exchange offices and banks are the most practical places to exchange currencies. These amenities may be found in popular tourist destinations and big cities. To guarantee you get a fair exchange rate, it is important to exchange your money at authorized businesses.

- **Cash vs. Cards:** While credit and debit cards are becoming popular in bigger places like hotels, restaurants, and stores, cash is still generally accepted in Uzbekistan, particularly for smaller transactions and in more rural locations. Carrying cash is usually a smart idea, especially in smaller towns and rural regions.

- **ATMs:** International credit cards like Visa and Mastercard are accepted at many ATMs, which are widespread in large cities. However, it's crucial to keep in mind that ATMs may not be as prevalent in smaller towns and rural locations, so it's best to withdraw enough cash while it's possible.

- **Currency Restrictions:** Uzbekistani som import and export are both prohibited. It is essential to confirm compliance with the rules by looking up the currency laws of both your own country and Uzbekistan.

- **Currency Exchange Advice:** It's best to carry modest denominations of UZS when exchanging money since it might be difficult to get change for bigger notes, particularly in more upscale locations. Keep your exchange receipts in case you need to exchange any remaining UZS after you leave the country.

Banking Hours: In Uzbekistan, the average banking hours are from 9:00 AM to 5:00 PM, Monday through Friday. It's advisable to verify the exact branch's operation hours, however, some banks could be open on Saturdays for a few hours as well.

- **International Banks:** In Uzbekistan, notably in Tashkent, there are branches of international financial institutions including HSBC, Standard Chartered, and National Bank of Pakistan. Account holders may also be able to get foreign exchange and international money transfers from these institutions.

- **Traveler's checks:** In Uzbekistan, they are often not frequently recognized. For your financial requirements, it is advised to carry both cash and cards.

To prevent any problems with card use or possible card blockages due to strange transactions, it is important to let your bank or credit card provider know about your trip intentions to Uzbekistan. Keeping a list of crucial phone numbers for your bank or credit card company on hand is also a smart idea in case something goes wrong.

To reduce the danger of theft or fraud, always use care while handling your money and be aware of your surroundings.

Getting Around in Uzbekistan

You have a variety of alternatives for getting to Uzbekistan when it comes to transportation that may help you get around and get where you need to go. Here are a few of the typical transportation options in Uzbekistan:

- **Domestic flights** are a practical and efficient means of covering great distances inside Uzbekistan. There are several domestic airports in the nation, including those at Urgench, Samarkand, Bukhara, and Tashkent. The national carrier that runs domestic flights is Uzbekistan Airways.

- **Trains:** Major cities and towns are connected by an extensive rail network in Uzbekistan. The railroad system provides a convenient and reasonably priced means of transportation. A speedier alternative for travel is the high-speed Afrosiyob railway, which runs between Tashkent, Samarkand, and Bukhara. Express trains and sluggish nighttime trains are among the additional trains.

- **Shared Taxis:** Also referred to as "marshrutkas," shared taxis are a well-liked form of local and short-distance transportation. These are usually minivans or automobiles that follow predetermined routes and may be waved down while driving. Taxis that can accommodate many passengers and have flexible departure schedules are known as shared taxis.

- **Buses:** In Uzbekistan, buses are a typical means of transportation. You may find both local buses and long-distance buses, and they link numerous cities and towns. While long-distance buses travel between large cities, local buses are more prevalent inside cities. It is wise to double-check the timetable and pick-up locations in advance.

- **Metro:** The metro system in Tashkent, the country's capital, provides a practical means of getting about the city. Both its stunning design and effective operation have made the Tashkent Metro a household name. It's a cheap and dependable way to move about Tashkent and go to the city's tourist hotspots.

- **Renting a vehicle** allows you the freedom to see Uzbekistan at your leisure. Major cities are home to several national and local vehicle rental firms. It's crucial to remember that driving conditions and road signs might change, thus it's advised that only experienced drivers use the roads.

- **Taxis:** In Uzbekistan's cities and towns, taxis are easily accessible. It's advisable to use authorized taxis with meters or to negotiate a fee before the trip begins. Some cities also provide ride-hailing services like Yandex and UzAuto, which provide dependable and convenient transportation.

- Planning your routes, taking into account journey times, and checking for any particular rules or laws are always smart ideas while using any means of transportation. Having local cash on hand is also a good idea, particularly when utilizing shared cabs or other forms of public transit.

Custom and Etiquettes

Understanding local traditions and etiquette is essential for a courteous and pleasurable trip to Uzbekistan. Here are some manners and traditions pointers to remember:

- The customary way to welcome someone in Uzbekistan is with a handshake and close eye contact. Depending on the time of day, use the proper greeting: "Assalomu alaykum" (hello) during the day and "Assalomu alaykum, kecha" (good evening) at night. It is usual to bow slightly when meeting elderly people or those in positions of power as a display of respect.

- **Dress Respectfully:** As a largely Muslim nation, in Uzbekistan, it is appropriate to wear modest clothing, particularly while visiting places of worship. Women should think about covering their shoulders and knees, and both sexes should refrain from donning exposing apparel. Additionally, it's usual to take off your shoes before entering a house or a mosque.

- **Respect for Elders:** Respect for elders is highly valued in Uzbek culture. Use proper words and actions to express respect for elderly people, and give them the upper hand in social settings.

- **Gift-giving:** When visiting someone's house in Uzbekistan, it's usual to deliver a modest gift.

Simple foods like tea, fruits, or sweets might be used as examples. As a demonstration of respect, use both hands to give over a gift. Gifts are often not opened right away, but rather later.

- **Dining Etiquette:** It's customary to take off your shoes before entering a house or traditional restaurant in Uzbekistan. Because traditional Uzbek meals are often eaten with hands, wash your hands before the meal. It's traditional to leave a tiny quantity of food on your plate to indicate that you have eaten enough meals, and it's polite to sample a bit of everything that is being provided.

- When photographing people, particularly in more private or religious contexts, they always get their consent. It's crucial to appreciate those who decline since they may have other preferences. In certain circumstances, such as at museums or historical places, photography may be restricted.

- **Religious places:** It's crucial to dress modestly and follow local norms while visiting mosques, mausoleums, or other religious places. Never engage in disruptive conduct or loud discussions, and always ask permission before entering any prohibited areas.

- **Language:** Learning a few simple words in the local tongue, such as "thank you" and "please," is valued and will help you get along well with the population. Russian is commonly spoken and understood, particularly in tourist regions, despite Uzbek being the official language.

You may demonstrate respect for Uzbek traditions and culture and foster good relationships with the people by adhering to these practices and manners. It's important to keep in mind that having a pleasant and fulfilling time in Uzbekistan depends on being kind, open-minded, and culturally aware.

Language and Communication

The Turkic language family includes Uzbek, which is the official language of Uzbekistan. But, particularly in metropolitan areas and among the older generation, Russian is also widely spoken and utilized as a lingua franca. The following are some crucial details about language and communication in Uzbekistan:

- Even though it's not required, knowing a few fundamental Uzbek words will substantially improve your relationships and demonstrate respect for the local way of life. We like simple salutations like "Assalomu alaykum" (hello) and "Rahmat" (thank you). Even if you just know a few words of their language, locals will usually appreciate your attempt.

- Russian is still a language that is widely spoken and understood, especially in urban areas, tourist hotspots, and among older generations. Both Russian and Uzbek are used to write a lot of menus, menu signs, and governmental documents. Knowing Russian may be useful for communication, particularly while interacting with authorities, at stores, or in transit hubs.

- Although younger generations and those employed in the tourist sector may speak English with some fluency, English is not generally spoken in Uzbekistan. English-speaking employees are more prevalent in hotels, bigger eateries, and tourist destinations. However, contact in English could be scarce outside of these regions.

- **Phrasebook or Translation App:** To aid overcome the language barrier, it is essential to carry a phrasebook or have a translation app close at hand. You may use these tools to help you grasp popular words, get directions, and have basic conversations. This may be especially helpful in more rural locations where English might not be as common.

- **Non-Verbal Communication:** Even when language abilities are limited, non-verbal communication may be crucial to communication. To communicate your message or comprehend others, use body language, facial emotions, and hand gestures. Always be aware of local customs and make sure your gestures are suitable and courteous.

- **Politeness and tolerance** are essential when dealing with linguistic obstacles. Be prepared to repeat or restate your statements if necessary, and speak slowly and clearly. It's very uncommon for locals to be kind and helpful, so don't be afraid to ask for help or explanation while speaking.

- Written Translations: If you come across written content in Russian or Uzbek that you don't understand, translation services are accessible in bigger cities or via mobile applications. These may assist you in understanding menus, signage, and other written materials.

Useful Uzbekistan Phrases

Hello: "Assalomu alaykum"

(ah-sah-LOH-moo ah-LAHY-koom)

Thank you: "Rahmat" (RAH-maht)

Yes: "Ha" (HAH)

No: "Yo'q" (YOHK)

Please: "Iltimos" (il-TEE-mohs)

Excuse me: "Kechirasiz"

(kech-ee-RAH-siz)

Sorry: "Uzr" (OOZR)

Goodbye: "Xayr" (HAYR)

How are you?: "Qalaysiz?"

(qa-LAY-siz)

I'm fine, thank you: "Yaxshi,

rahmat" (YAHK-shee, RAH-maht)

Do you speak English?: "Siz inglizcha gapirasizmi?" (siz een-GLIZ-cha gah-pee-RAH-siz-mee)

Where is...?: "...qayerda?" (...ka-YER-da)

How much does it cost?: "Necha pul?" (ne-CHA pool)

Can you help me?: "Yordam berasizmi?" (YOR-dahm beh-RAH-siz-mee)

I don't understand: "Tushunmadim" (toosh-oon-MAH-deem)

Helpful Phone Numbers and Websites

Emergency Numbers:

Police: 102

Ambulance: 103

Fire Department: 101

Tourist Information:

Uzbekistan State Committee for Tourism Development: +998 71 233 28 28

Website: https://www.uzbekistan.travel/en

Transportation:

Uzbekistan Airways (National
Airline): +998 71 140 02 00
Website:
https://www.uzairways.com/en

Uzbekistan Railways: +998 71 238
28 28
Website: http://railway.uz/en

Tashkent International Airport:
+998 71 140 28 00
Website:
http://www.uzairports.uz/en/

Tourist Services and Information:

Uzbekistan Tourism Information Centers:

Tashkent Tourism Information Center: +998 71 256 07 27
Samarkand Tourism Information Center: +998 66 233 33 10
Bukhara Tourism Information Center: +998 65 221 30 30
Visit Uzbekistan (Official Tourism Website):
https://www.visituzbekistan.travel/en

It is advised that you carry a hard copy of these phone numbers in addition to saving them to your phone. To surf websites and get the most recent information when visiting Uzbekistan, it's also a good idea to have an internet connection or a local SIM card.

Packing Tips and Traveler's Hacks

- Pack season-appropriate, lightweight, and breathable clothes. Consider wearing layers of clothes in Uzbekistan because of the country's scorching summers and chilly winters. When visiting holy locations, modest clothing is advised.

- Carry good walking shoes since you'll probably be roaming around cities and historical places. Also, for warmer weather, think about bringing sandals or flip-flops.

- Travel adapter: Since Type C and Type F electrical outlets are used in Uzbekistan, you'll need one to charge your electronics.

- Travel papers: Keep hard copies or digital versions of your passport, visa, travel insurance, and other crucial papers with you at all times. Having a copy of your hotel bookings and emergency contact information is also a smart idea.

- Prescription drugs and basic first aid supplies should be brought along, along with any required bandages, antiseptic cream, and painkillers.

- Pack sunscreen, a hat, and sunglasses to shield yourself from the sun's rays since Uzbekistan may experience severe sunshine.

- Carry bug repellent with you to prevent mosquito bites since they may be common in certain regions, especially in the summer.

- Travel Lock: When traveling, a tiny travel lock may provide an additional degree of protection for your baggage.

Travelers' Tips:

- Carry a reusable water bottle: Hydration is crucial, so carrying a reusable bottle can help you save money and lessen the amount of plastic garbage you produce.

- Learn some fundamental Uzbek or Russian words and phrases to help you communicate with people and get through everyday situations.

- Carry small dollars and coins in the local currency. These will come in useful for tipping, buying snacks, and utilizing public transit.

- Keep in touch with a local SIM card to have access to data and make local calls, which may be helpful for communication and navigation.

- Keep an eye out for cultural norms: To respect the local culture and prevent inadvertent transgressions, familiarize yourself with local traditions and etiquette.

- Investigate your alternatives for getting around: To save time and money, check out the routes and timetables for the local public transportation system in advance.

- Be careful while eating street food: While it may be tempting, find vendors that follow excellent cleanliness procedures to prevent foodborne infections.

VIII. PERFECT ITINERARIES FOR UZBEKISTAN TRAVEL

5-Day Schedule:

1st day: Tashkent

- Discover the attractions of the capital of Tashkent, including Independence Square, Chorsu Bazaar, and Khast Imam Complex.
- Learn about the rich history and culture of the nation by visiting the State Museum of History of Uzbekistan.

Next day: Samarkand

- Get on a fast train and travel to Samarkand.
- Spend the day admiring Shah-i-Zinda, Gur-e-Amir Mausoleum, and the majestic Registan Square.
- Visit the Bibi-Khanym Mosque and the Ulugh Beg Observatory.

3rd day: Bukhara

- Drive or take a train to Bukhara.
- Learn about Bukhara's ancient center, which is designated by UNESCO and contains the Ark of Bukhara, the Kalyan Minaret, and the Poi Kalon Complex.
- Visit the regional artisan studios and stroll around the lovely old town.

4th day: Khiva

- Visit the wonderfully preserved ancient city of Khiva.
- Explore the Kunya-Ark Citadel and the Juma Mosque as you meander through the Itchan Kala fortress's winding alleyways.
- From the city walls, take in the sunset.

5th day: Tashkent

- Come back to Tashkent.
- Visit the city's contemporary area, which includes the Navoi Opera and Ballet Theater and Amir Timur Square.
- Investigate the neighborhood markets for any last-minute purchases and mementos.

7-Day Schedule:

Continue with the 5-day schedule and add the following:

Sixth day: Shakhrisabz

- Visit Tamerlane's birthplace, Shakhrisabz, for the day.
- Discover the Kok Gumbaz Mosque, the Dorut-Tilavat Ensemble, and the Ak-Saray Palace.

7th day: Tashkent

- Spend an additional day in Tashkent seeing sights you may have missed or discovering the lively districts and parks of the city.
- At reputable eateries, unwind while indulging in regional food.

Itinerary for 14 days:

Continue with the 7-day schedule and add the following:

8th to 11th day: Fergana Valley

- Visit the lovely Fergana Valley.
- Discover the rich cultural legacy, silk manufacture, and ceramics of the towns of Kokand, Margilan, and Rishtan.
- Visit regional bazaars, artisanal studios, and historical locations.

Day 12–14: Regions of Nukus and Khorezm

- Fly to Nukus, the regional capital of the independent Karakalpakstan.
- Visit the renowned Savitsky Museum to see its distinctive collection of avant-garde Soviet art.
- Discover the historic fortifications of Khorezm, including Ayaz Kala and Toprak Kala.
- Visit the Aral Sea and the Muynak Ship Graveyard to round up your journey.

These itineraries provide a taste of the many historical and cultural sites in Uzbekistan. Always examine each destination's opening hours, available modes of transportation, and seasonal restrictions. You are welcome to change the itineraries to suit your tastes and available time.

IX. FINAL THOUGHTS AND RECOMMENDATIONS

It's time to take stock of your experiences and make plans for the future as your trip to Uzbekistan draws to a conclusion. For a book conclusion and some suggestions to round off your tour, see below:

Your trip across Uzbekistan has been an exciting study of both historic secrets and cutting-edge activities. You've delved into the rich tapestry of Uzbekistan's culture, history, and landscapes, from the busy streets of Tashkent to the grandeur of Samarkand, the ancient allure of Bukhara, the charming old town of Khiva, and the natural splendor of the Nuratau Mountains and Fergana Valley.

The Silk Road's history, the UNESCO World Heritage Sites, local crafts, and energetic festivals have all had an impact. The friendliness and kindness of the Uzbek people have added to the quality of your trip.

Consider the amazing views you've seen, the tastes you've had, and the relationships you've established with the locals as you come to the end of your journey. A place that provides a window into its historic past and a look into its developing future, Uzbekistan has emerged as a hidden treasure.

Recommendations:

- Explore more: If you have the chance, think about looking into seeing more of Central Asia. The neighboring nations of Kyrgyzstan, Tajikistan, and Kazakhstan each offer distinctive landscapes, customs, and tourist attractions.

- Share Your Experience: Tell others about your travel experiences in Uzbekistan. Share your experiences, pictures, and tales on social media, travel blogs, and with friends and family. Encourage people to explore this fascinating nation's attractions.

- Explore Uzbekistan's history, culture, and customs in more detail through reading books and literature. Examine writings that highlight the history of the Silk Road, Central Asian culture, and travel accounts.

- Stay Connected: Keep an eye on changes in the travel and tourism sector in Uzbekistan. The nation may develop new attractions and experiences as it continues to develop and change, luring travelers there in the future.

- Come Back for More: Future travel to Uzbekistan should be considered. Because of its constantly changing scenery, there is always something new to learn and experience. Return to discover off-the-beaten-path locales or revisit your favorite places.

Keep in mind that your Discovery of the world's treasures is only starting with your trip to Uzbekistan. Accept the memories you've made and use them as motivation to go out on new experiences, learn about new people and cultures, and take in the beauty of our unique globe.

Made in the USA
Las Vegas, NV
02 December 2023

81998503R00087